Other books by Ingri & Edgar Parin d'Aulaire

ABRAHAM LINCOLN

BENJAMIN FRANKLIN

BUFFALO BILL

COLUMBUS

LEIF THE LUCKY

POCAHONTAS

Published by Beautiful Feet Books
1306 Mill Street
San Luis Obispo, CA 93401
www.bfbooks.com
800-889-1978

GEORGE
WASHINGTON

Lithographed on stone
in five colors by the authors
and printed by offset lithography
in the United States of America
All rights reserved

The Library of Congress has cataloged this work as follows:

D'Aulaire, Ingri, 1904–
    George Washington, by Ingri & Edgar Parin d'Aulaire.   1st ed. Garden City,
N.Y., Doubleday, Doran, 1936.

    [55] p. illus. (part col.) 32 cm.

    Summary: A simple biography of Washington, telling of the major events in
his life and stressing the upbringing that endowed him with the qualities of
leadership.

    1. Washington, George, 1732-1799—Juvenile literature. [1. Washington,
George, 1732-1799] I. D'Aulaire, Edgar Parin, 1898-   joint author. II.
Title.

E312.66.D37 1936	973.4'1'0924	36-27417
	[B] [92]	MARC
Library of Congress	[r86]rev2	AC

ISBN: 978-0-9643803-1-8 Paperback

GEORGE
WASHINGTON

by

INGRI & EDGAR
PARIN D'AULAIRE

Published by Beautiful Feet Books

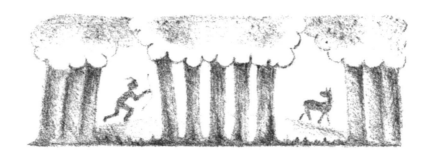

VIRGINIA was once a wilderness. Wild beasts lived there, and swift Indians ran through grass and swamps. In the fall the Indians went to the shore and pitched their camps on the bluff where Pope's Creek falls into the great Potomac River. Here they fished and caught oysters, and threw the empty shells around their wigwams. The shells piled up and up, until at last the top of the bluff became an oyster-shell hill.

Then across the sea came the men from England and chased the Indians away. The Englishmen settled on the land, and their king ruled over Virginia. One of these men from England was John Washington. He chose the land around the oyster-shell hill, where he built a home for his family. He cleared much wilderness and made a big farm. And here on Wakefield Farm, more than two hundred years ago, his grandson's son, George Washington, was born.

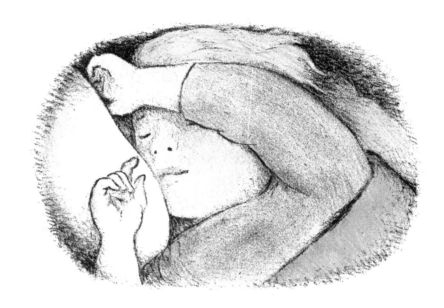

HE was born in a little red brick house that his father had built on the oyster-shell hill. By that time so much land had been cleared that the wilderness was far in the distance, hidden in the blue haze. Horses and cows had their pasture where wild beasts had lived, and black slaves worked on the Indian hunting grounds. For the hunting grounds had become great fields of grain and tobacco. George heard about the Indians from his father when they walked around together looking after the farm, which was now so big that they called it a plantation. And he learned that all the family were both fed and dressed by the crops that grew in the fields.

THE tobacco leaves were sent on ships to England. There they were exchanged for beautiful clothing, like the suit he wore himself, and for other fine things they did not yet know how to make in Virginia. The humming birds shot through the air, the wild turkey clucked to her chicks, and little George dug and planted in a corner of his mother's garden. He had only himself to play with, for his sister Betty was still a baby and the children on the next plantation lived very far away. It was much too far to walk, and he was still too small to ride a pony.

As soon as his feet could reach the stirrups his father gave him a pony, and he began to learn to ride. At first the pony jumped and shook itself. But George hung onto the mane and did not show that he was afraid. So it was not long before he could sit firmly in the saddle and hold the bridle right. Then he and the pony were friends, and he rode with his mother and father to visit the neighboring plantations.

By this time too the Washington family had left the oyster-shell hill. They were living at Mount Vernon, another plantation his father owned higher up on the great Potomac River. And George now had some little brothers to play with and look after.

IN the evening his
mother called the children together, and they all
sat quietly around the fireplace in the living
room. She told them stories from the Holy
Bible, and on the shiny tiles of the fireplace there
were painted pictures of the stories she told.
Thus George learned his Bible, and he learned
to be good and honest and never tell a lie.

WHEN George Washington was old enough to go to school his father decided to move from Mount Vernon to another plantation he had bought. In a big carriage the whole family drove through deep forests. Tall trees shut out the light, and from behind the trunks birds and beasts peered curiously at the travelers. But George did not see any Indians, for the Indians lived still deeper in the wilderness. Even so he had many adventures on his journey, for the roads were bad and it was difficult to travel in those days. Every now and then the wheels stuck in a mudhole, or a rotten tree fell straight across the road. Then the horses jumped over the tree and quite forgot that the carriage could not jump too. But the Washingtons reached Ferry Farm, on the Rappahannock River, safely. That was their new home.

Now George Washington was taught to read and write, and he also learned to dance. For every boy and girl in those days had to know how to dance.

One day two young and handsomely dressed gentlemen arrived. They were his grown-up half brothers. He had never seen them before, for they had been away to school in England. At first George was so shy that he almost stumbled over his own feet, but it was not long before he and his brothers were friends. He loved his oldest brother, Lawrence, most. Lawrence was an officer, and George wanted to be an officer too. So he played that he was general and drumbeater and scared all the chickens when he led his sister and brothers to great and glorious wars.

HE was big enough now to saddle his pony himself in the morning and ride to school in Fredericksburg Town. He was tall and strong, and rode his horse better than any other boy of his age, and he beat them all in races and games. His friends said he was so strong that he could throw a coin across the Rappahannock River. At school he was clever too, for he was eager to learn and listened to his teacher. In his copy book he wrote down all the rules a gentleman should know. He wrote:

In the presence of others sing not to yourself
nor drum with your fingers nor feet.

Give not your advice without being asked.

Undertake not what you cannot perform,
but be careful to keep your promise.

Let your countenance be pleasant,
but in serious matters somewhat grave.

GEORGE Washington was only eleven years old when he lost his father. Then his mother was not very rich, so he could not go to school in England as his half brothers had done. He had to learn how to provide for himself. He became serious and studious and taught himself many things. Because he was clever at arithmetic and loved outdoor life, he began to study surveying. He wanted to go into the wilderness, where only the Indians lived, and measure up the unknown land. He measured up the fields of the plantation, and till late into the evening, while the fireflies glittered over the fields, he worked with his compass and ruler and drew maps of the land he had measured.

H

IS half brother, Lawrence, was rich, for he had inherited Mount Vernon, and he asked George to come and stay with him there for a while. Lawrence always had many elegant guests, and when George came they all liked him because he was bright and well brought up. He watched them all and learned how to bow and take snuff and converse politely. He was so tall now that he almost looked like a grown-up man. And nobody was better than he at riding and hunting. Once, at a fox hunt at Mount Vernon, he met Lord Fairfax, the richest man in Virginia. After that Lord Fairfax always wanted him along when he went hunting. He thought so much of George that he asked him to become one of his surveyors and measure up his great lands that stretched far into the wilderness.

TOGETHER with the other surveyors George Washington set off. He worked hard and made maps of the land, and at night he slept on the bare ground. Often wind and rain tore the tent from over his head, but he did not mind, for he was strong as a bear. He rode over high hills and deep valleys and through endless forests. Far, far away from other people he came to some small farms. There lived the backwoodsmen. Their children had never seen a stranger before, and were almost as shy as rabbits. But George knew the ways of his own little brothers and soon made friends with them. Still deeper in the forest he met the trappers, who lived by catching fur-bearing animals. They had not brought their children along, for here the land of the Indians began.

ONE day he met a tribe of Indians coming from war with scalps at their belts. George Washington and his friends gave them presents, and the Indians danced their war dance for them. They were friendly with the surveyors, and smoked peace pipes with them. This was the first time George Washington had seen a tribe of Indians, and he thought their war dance very funny. But now the surveyors had reached the end of the Fairfax lands and were ready to return. Lord Fairfax was very much pleased with the maps George Washington had made. Other people, too, asked him to survey their land, and soon he was made surveyor for the whole county. So he traveled all over Virginia and got to know the wilderness and the ways of the Indians better than most other men. His free time he spent at Mount Vernon. There Lawrence taught him to be a soldier, and when George Washington was twenty years old he became an officer.

For some years now French soldiers had been coming from Canada down the Ohio River. They had built fortresses, made friends with many Indian tribes, and with the Indians they were chasing away the Virginia backwoodsmen. The governor sent for George Washington, for he had heard about his courage and skill. He wanted him to try to push his way through the wilderness and take a message to the French commander, asking the French to leave the Virginians in peace. With a few men George Washington set off at once. He dodged many perils, till deep in the wilderness he met "Halfking," an Indian chieftain. They became such good friends that Halfking and his braves led George Washington and his men on hidden trails until they came to some log houses surrounded by a strong wooden fence. That was the French fortress.

Late in the fall George Washington came back to Williamsburg, where the Governor of Virginia lived in a palace. George was worn and tired. Hostile Indians had attacked him and he had almost drowned in an icy river. But he had come through all the dangers and returned with the French commander's answer. The governor received him in his beautiful palace and could not praise him enough. He gave him a higher rank in the army, and the young George Washington was honored by everyone in Virginia. At the gates of the governor's palace the great and small stood to bow and to greet him. But from the message he had brought back it was easy to see that the French wanted part of Virginia. So the governor gave George Washington several hundred soldiers and sent him out to keep the French and Indians away.

For four years George Washington fought. Valiantly he defended the backwoodsmen and their wives and children against the Indian raids. The English king sent a great army to chase away the French soldiers and the Indian tribes. In a straight line the red-coated English soldiers marched into the wilderness. George Washington told them they ought to hide themselves behind trees and bushes instead of marching that way, but they would not listen. So when the Indian warriors fell upon them from their hiding-places behind the trees, the whole army was beaten. George Washington's coat was pierced by many bullets, but he was unharmed. Later the English king sent a still bigger army, and together with George Washington and the other Virginians the English soldiers succeeded in chasing away the French and the Indian tribes, and they never came back.

Now George Washington was the hero of all Virginia. He hurried back to Williamsburg, for there a pretty young widow was waiting for him. This was Martha Custis. She had promised to marry him as soon as the war was over.

They had a gorgeous wedding, and from far and near wedding guests came. When George Washington and his bride danced, all the wedding guests admired them. The bride was just as small and plump and gay as the groom was tall and slim and serious.

Martha had two children, Patsy and John Custis, and George Washington became their new father. With his wife and children he traveled to Mount Vernon, which he now owned, for his brother Lawrence had died.

FOR fifteen years Washington lived happily at Mount Vernon. He brought up the children and took care of his plantation. Every year he cleared more land, until Mount Vernon was at last like a little kingdom. His people needed neither shops nor towns, for they made everything at home. In one house sat the spinners, in one the weavers, in one the seamstresses. There was a blacksmith shop, a carpenter shop and a mason shop. The storehouses were filled with food from gardens and fields and with fish from the great Potomac River. George Washington was everywhere, and his hundreds of slaves and servants kept everything spick and span and in beautiful order.

THE house was always full of guests. There were many children and gay parties, but there also came serious men to talk with Washington. They talked about the difficulties the colonies had with their mother country, England. England was so far away that the English king could not know how very different things were in the American colonies. Thus many misunderstandings arose. The English king wanted the colonists to pay taxes which the Americans thought were unjust. And he would not let them help make their own laws. At last, the people of Boston refused to obey him, and he sent his soldiers, the Redcoats, to close the port and rule the town. Then everybody in the thirteen American colonies grew so angry that they made up their minds to fight together against the Redcoats.

THE Americans all agreed that George Washington was the wisest and bravest soldier they had. They asked him to be their commander-in-chief and lead them in defense of their rights and liberties. George Washington mounted his horse and, accompanied by some of his officers, set off on the long journey to Boston. He had not gone far when a messenger came riding toward him bringing news of the battle of Bunker Hill. So bravely had the New Englanders fought that the strong force of Redcoats had retired into Boston and did not dare to come out.

"The liberties of the country are safe," cried Washington when he heard how gallantly the New Englanders had fought. And he and his officers hurried on.

On the common of Cambridge, outside Boston, General Washington took command of his army. It was a strange army, for his men were not soldiers, but farmers and hunters. They were brave, but whenever they wanted to see their farms and their children they ran home, and Washington never knew how many men he had. Patiently he set to work to make them good soldiers, and after some months he had them so well trained that they were able to force the Redcoats out of Boston. But that did not end the war. The king sent still more soldiers from England, until there were so many of them that General Washington could not keep them from taking New York.

THIS was the time that the "Liberty Bell" rang over America. The colonists had decided that they would not be part of England any more because the English king would not try to understand their troubles. They would be free. On the fourth of July, 1776, they declared their independence. They were determined to get their rights and their liberty. Washington led his soldiers through all dangers and difficulties. He retreated with his army when he saw he could not win, but whenever he had a chance he attacked. When the Redcoats thought they had beaten him he returned. Through snowstorm and ice he came back with his men across the Delaware River. He surprised the Redcoats at Trenton, and won a victory.

For several years the war went on. Sometimes the Redcoats won, and sometimes Washington.

THE American soldiers bore much hardship. They were ragged and hungry and cold. Hardest was the winter in Valley Forge. They were so cold and hungry that they wanted to give up and go home. But Washington did not give up, and he kept them together. He starved with them and froze with them, and his soldiers loved him so much that they stayed for his sake. From farms and towns near-by, grown-ups and children came to the camp. They brought butter and ham and potatoes, and all the other food they could spare. All the way from Europe officers came to help Washington win. From France came Lafayette to fight at his side, and from Germany came General von Steuben to help him train his men.

WHEN spring came at Valley Forge Washington mounted his snow-white horse and led his army against the English. At Monmouth in New Jersey they fought a big battle. So well trained were the American soldiers now, that the Redcoats could only save themselves by flight in the darkness of the night. When the King of France heard this he sent a great fleet and an army to help General Washington make an end to the war. With his French and American soldiers Washington marched to Yorktown in Virginia, where Lord Cornwallis was staying with a great part of the Redcoats. The French put their ships like a chain in front of the town so nobody could escape, and Washington with his men attacked from land. For three weeks they fought. Then Lord Cornwallis could not fight any more. He came out from the town, handed over his sword and surrendered with his whole army.

BUT still for a long while the Redcoats stayed in New York. At last the peace was signed, and the Redcoats made ready to sail in their ships. They were no longer enemies, and before they sailed the English admiral asked General Washington to dine with him on his ship. When Washington came he was greeted as the first man of a free and independent country. The Redcoats bowed, and their cannons thundered as a salute. Then they took leave of each other as friends and Washington rode home to Mount Vernon.

Washington came home to Mount Vernon on Christmas Day. At the door stood Martha, his wife, with a little girl and boy at her side. They were her grandchildren, who had come to live with her at Mount Vernon. With beaming faces the slaves and servants, too, welcomed their master home. His tired horse got rest in the stable, and his general's uniform was hung away. As before the war, the house was filled with guests. All his friends and relatives and also many people he did not know came to thank him for what he had done for America.

Now Washington was happy. He walked peacefully over his fields, where the slaves were singing and working. He watched the plants shoot up from the soil in the strong Virginia sun, while his stepgrandchildren played around him. Once again he was "Farmer Washington," and that was what he liked best to be.

Bᴜᴛ the Americans needed a man to rule over them instead of the English king, and they said: "George Washington led us to freedom, he is the first man in the country, and he shall be our president." Never before had there been such celebrations in the country as when George Washington drove to New York and was inaugurated as the first President of the United States of America. For eight years he was President and led his countrymen wisely and justly, and the country grew strong and rich. It was he who founded and planned the town of Washington, with the Capitol and the White House. And all his countrymen honored and loved him.

The little boy from the lone Virginia plantation
had become the Father
of His Country.

Any biography of the life of George Washington will naturally bring up for young children the simple question of how it came to be that the Father of our Country owned slaves. How is it possible that a man of Washington's integrity, who fought so selflessly for liberty and justice, could be involved in the lamentable institution of slavery? Though the answer is not simple, a few basic historic facts will help children understand this aspect of the Founder's life.

Washington inherited his first slaves at the tender age of eleven, upon the untimely death of his father. The young Washington was born into a culture of slavery that was supported by every institution around him including the church, the educational system, and the civil government. Slavery as an institution extended back in history to ancient times, and even the very philosophers that George would have studied in school—Aristotle, Plato, Cicero, and Seneca, accepted slavery as an inescapable reality of life. At age nineteen Washington took his only trip to foreign shores—to Barbados with his half-brother Lawrence—and even this experience would have reinforced in him that slavery was a normative part of life. Growing up in the plantation culture of Virginia, Washington would have had little opportunity to challenge or question the ethical nature of slavery itself.

While Washington had little occasion to reflect upon the evils of slavery in the early years of his life, by the time the colonies were agitating for independence from Great Britain, his view of slavery was being confronted and challenged. This was due not only to the language of freedom circulating in the colonies regarding the rights of man but also to the warm friendship he enjoyed with the Marquis de Lafayette—an ardent opponent of slavery. Indeed, the very language of the first draft of the Declaration of Independence included an initial provision for emancipation, calling the slave trade an "execrable commerce"—something that ought to be loathed and abhorred. During the time that Washington commanded the Continental troops in Boston, he was visited by America's first black woman poet, Phillis Wheatley. Phillis so admired Washington that she had written a moving tribute to him for his part in the colonies fight for independence. Washington was quite stirred by this and wrote the poet a heartfelt letter of thanks. It is intriguing to wonder how meeting this classically educated black woman may have inspired Washington's views for the future of freed black Americans. By these influences and many others too numerous to detail here, Washington came to the opinion that slavery must be abolished.

Ten years after the Declaration, writing to Robert Morris, Washington stated, "There is not a man living who wishes more sincerely than I do, to see a plan adopted for the abolition of slavery." Remarkably, Washington was able to confront the prejudices of his own times while fully realizing the economic repercussion this would have to the entire plantation South. In Washington's last will and testament, he directed his heirs to free all the slaves belonging to him upon the death of his wife Martha. This remarkable action set him apart from all the Founders and established once again his leadership and integrity. Phillis Wheatley's tribute to Washington lauds him for the sacrificial part he played in the struggle for freedom and independence in America. Though it was not his part to lead the charge in abolition, he faithfully played his part in establishing this nation as free and independent. The nation firmly built upon Washington's foundation did eventually do the work of emancipation. And in freeing his own slaves, Washington showed he was a half-century ahead of his time.

–Rea Berg, Publisher

Fixed are the eyes of nations on the scales,
For in their hopes Columbia's arm prevails.
Anon Britannia droops the pensive head,
While round increase the rising hills of dead.
Ah! Cruel blindness to Columbia's state!
Lament thy thirst of boundless power too late.
Proceed great chief, with virtue on thy side,
Thy ev'ry action let the goddess guide.
A crown, a mansion, and a throne that shine,
With gold unfading, WASHINGTON, be thine.

Excerpted from "To His Excellency, George Washington" by Phillis Wheatley